Play the Electronic Keyboard

Book 2

Nicholas Haines

By the same author
Play the Electronic Keyboard Book 1
Composing on the Electronic Keyboard Books 1 and 2

LONGMAN GROUP UK LIMITED
Longman House
Burnt Mill, Harlow, Essex CM20 2JE, England
and Associated Companies throughout the World

First published 1986

ISBN 0-582-22460-8

Set in 11/13pt Helvetica Regular (Lasercomp).

Printed and Bound in Great Britain at the Bath Press, Avon.

Acknowledgements

We are grateful to the following for permission to reproduce copyright songs:

ATV Music Ltd for *When I'm 64* by John Lennon and Paul McCartney; Box & Cox Publications Ltd for *I've got a lovely bunch of coconuts* by F. Heatherton © 1944 Irwin Dash Ltd Assigned to Box & Cox Ltd 1948; Virgin Music (Publishers) Ltd & Warner Bros Music Ltd for a simplified version of *Karma Chameleon* by O'Dowd, Moss, Hay, Craig, Picket © 1983 Virgin Music (Pubs) Ltd/Warner Bros Music Ltd.

Contents

UNIT 1

The G major scale

The notes which make up C major scale use only the white notes of the keyboard starting on the note C.

C major scale

Now play a scale starting on the note G still using only the white notes of the keyboard. You should hear one note which sounds out of place. It is F. To get the same scale pattern as you had for C major, you will have to play a black note – the one to the right of the F key.

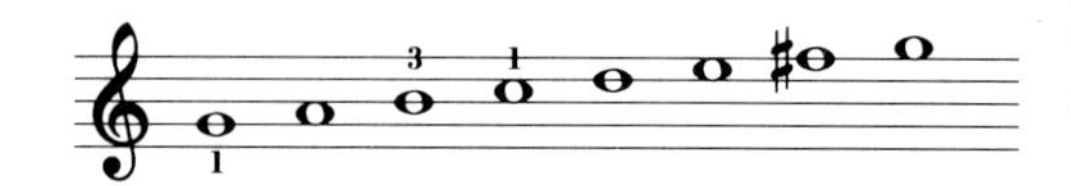

G major scale

The sharp sign ♯ written before a note tells you to play the very next key to the *right*.

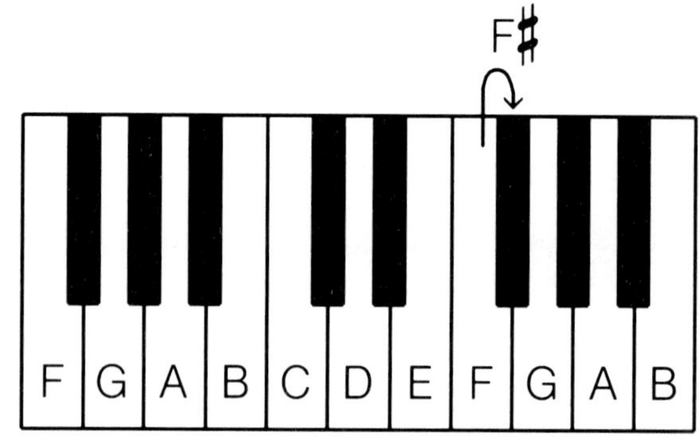

Key Signatures

In G major, the note F will normally be sharpened, i.e. played as F♯. Instead of writing a sharp sign in front of every F, a key signature is written at the beginning of every stave.

The key signature for G major is F♯. This tells you that every F must now be sharpened; this includes the other F notes on the treble clef.

1. Scales are important. They help you to exercise your fingers and give you a guide for fingering the keys. Practising scales can be fun if you accompany them with the auto-chords and rhythms.

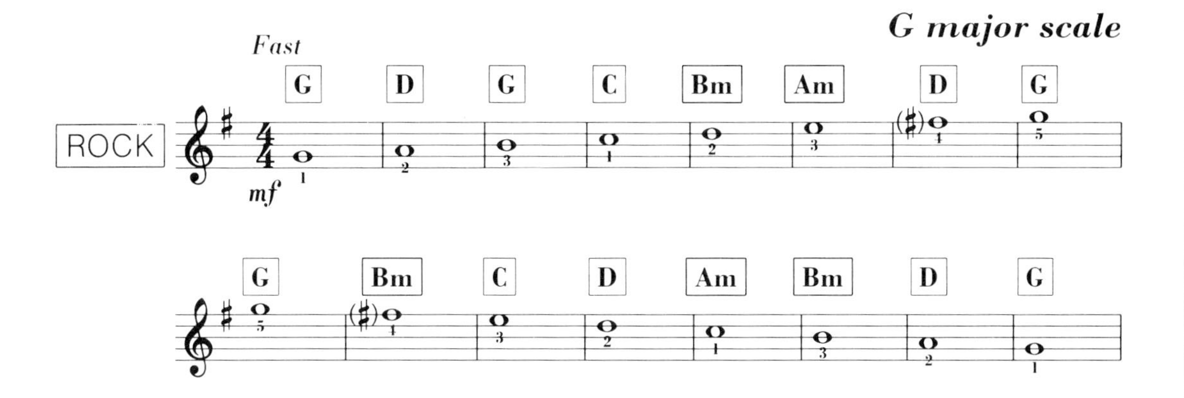

2. Choose a sustained instrumental sound such as a violin for this waltz melody. Don't forget the key signature of F♯.

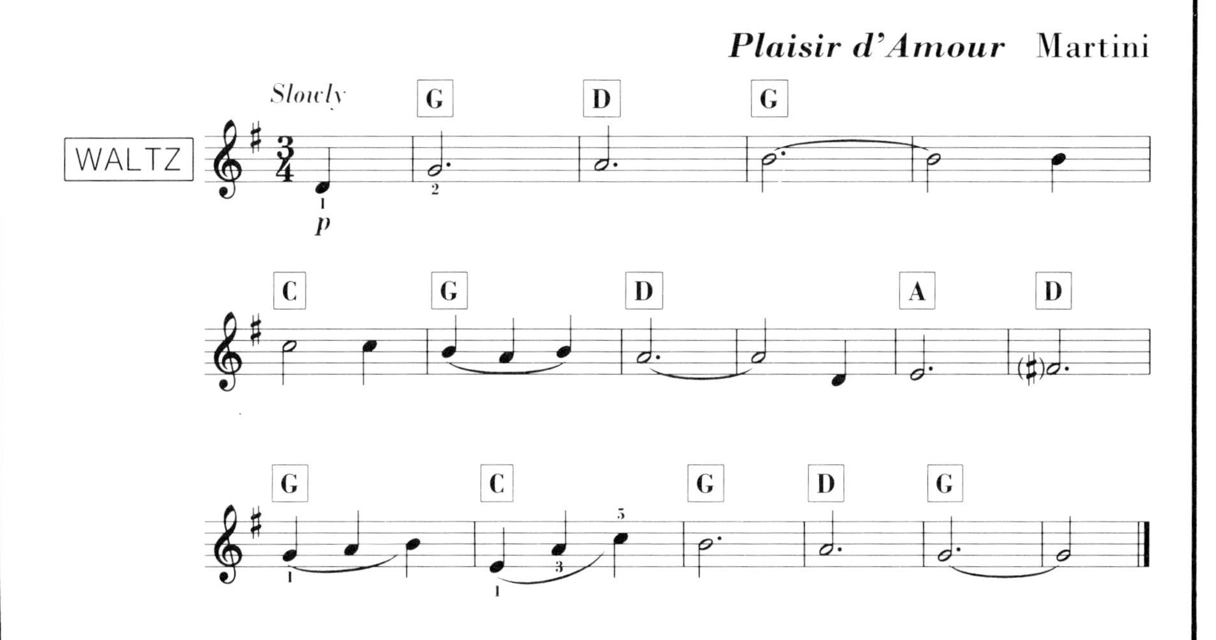

UNIT 2

Seventh chords

Seventh chords can add 'spice' to the accompaniment by adding another note on top of the basic chord.

Seventh chords are shown by a number '7' written after the chord letter, e.g. E7. Sevenths can be added to both major and minor chords. Here are two of the most usual ways of playing seventh chords on the auto-section of the keyboard. The actual method will depend on the make of keyboard that you play.

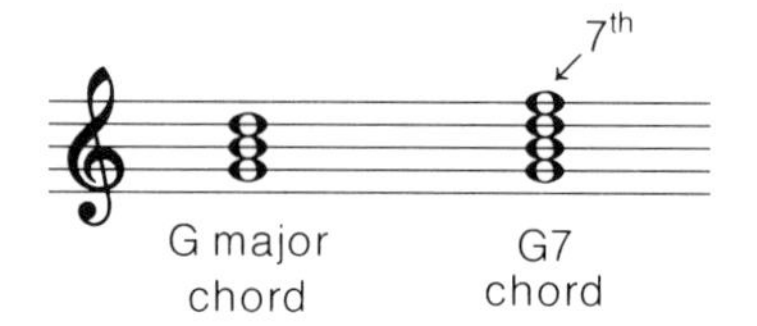

Major chord with 7th

Either play the letter name of the chord together with the white note to the left.

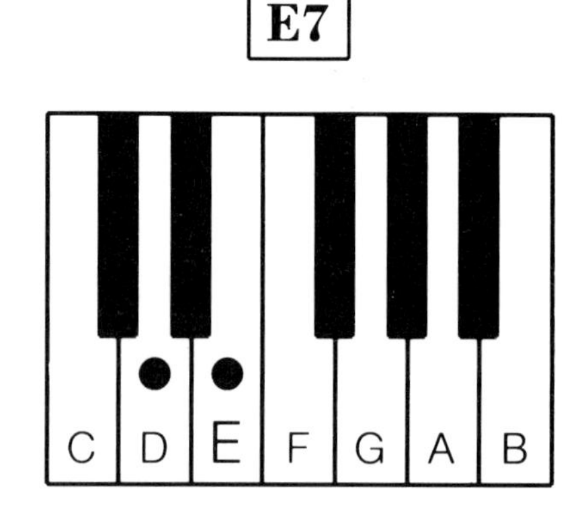

Or play the letter name of the chord together with two notes to the right.

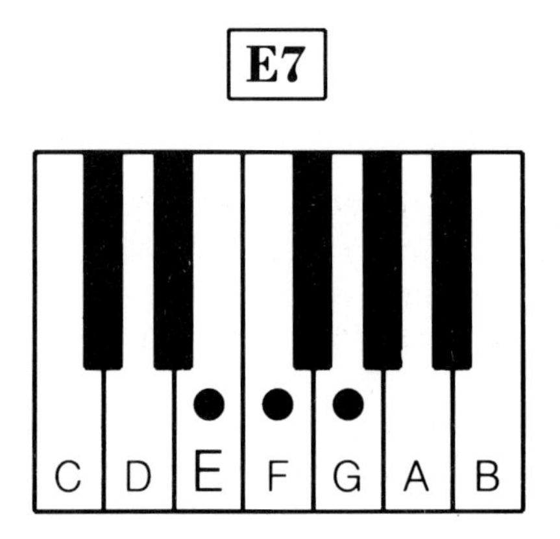

Minor chord with 7th

Either play the letter name of the chord together with the white and black notes to the left.

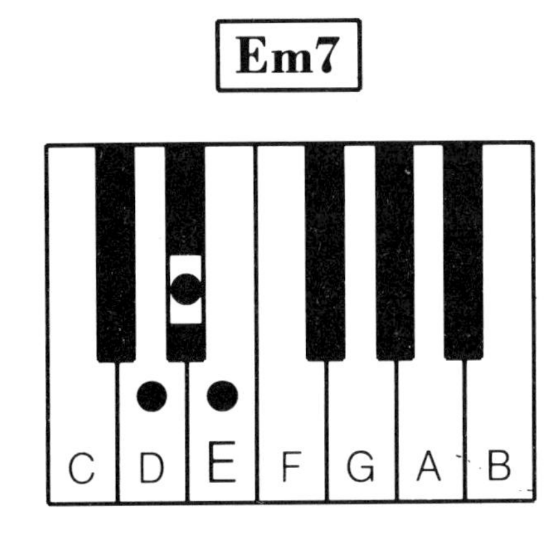

Or play the letter name of the chord together with three notes to the right.

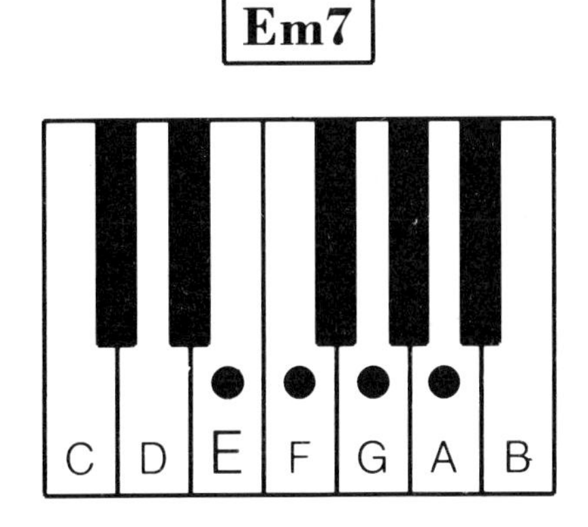

Check with your keyboard manual to see which method you need to use.

Playing without the auto-rhythm

You do not need to use the auto-rhythm all the time. Many pieces of music sound better without drums. Press the auto-chord button but not the synchro/start.

The chord and melody will sound but there will be no rhythmic accompaniment.

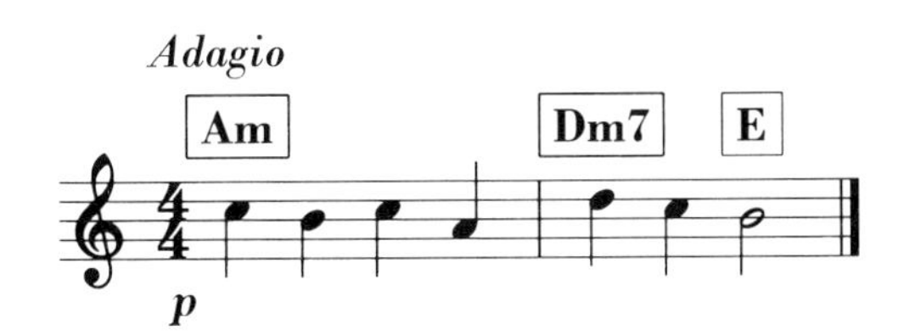

1. This chordal exercise uses four types of chord: major, minor, major with 7th, and minor with 7th. When you play each chord, make sure you press the auto-keys at the same time. Lift your fingers off immediately you have played the auto-keys.

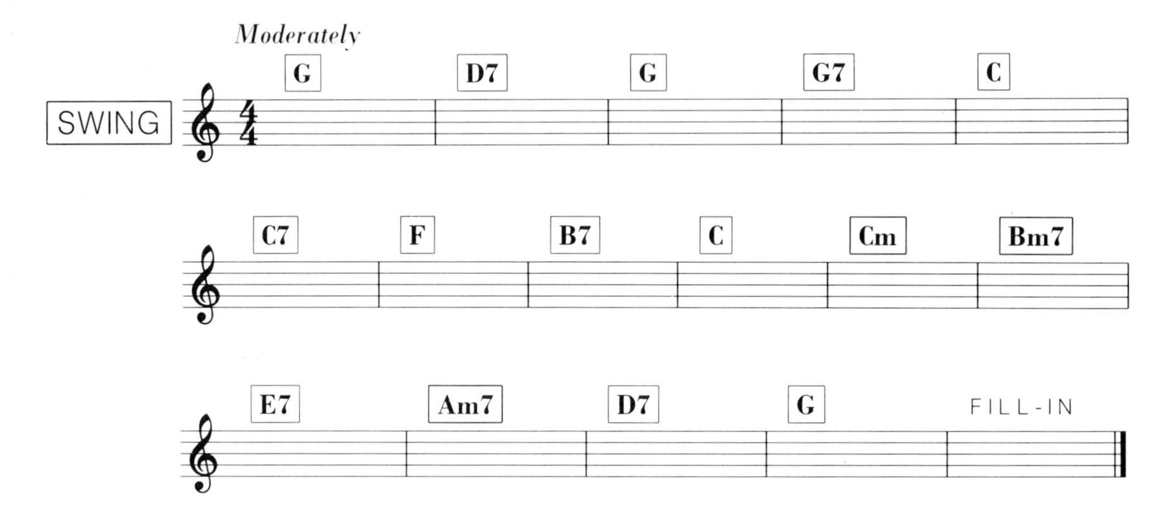

2. Play the carol *Away in a Manger* without any rhythmic accompaniment. Use the auto-chord feature but do not press the synchro/start button.

3. Do not be put off playing songs which seem to have a lot of notes. Practise the chords first on the auto-section. Then play the skeleton of the melody by missing out the quavers. When the simplified melody and auto-chords are learnt, add the quavers. Try this method with the song *Karma Chameleon*.

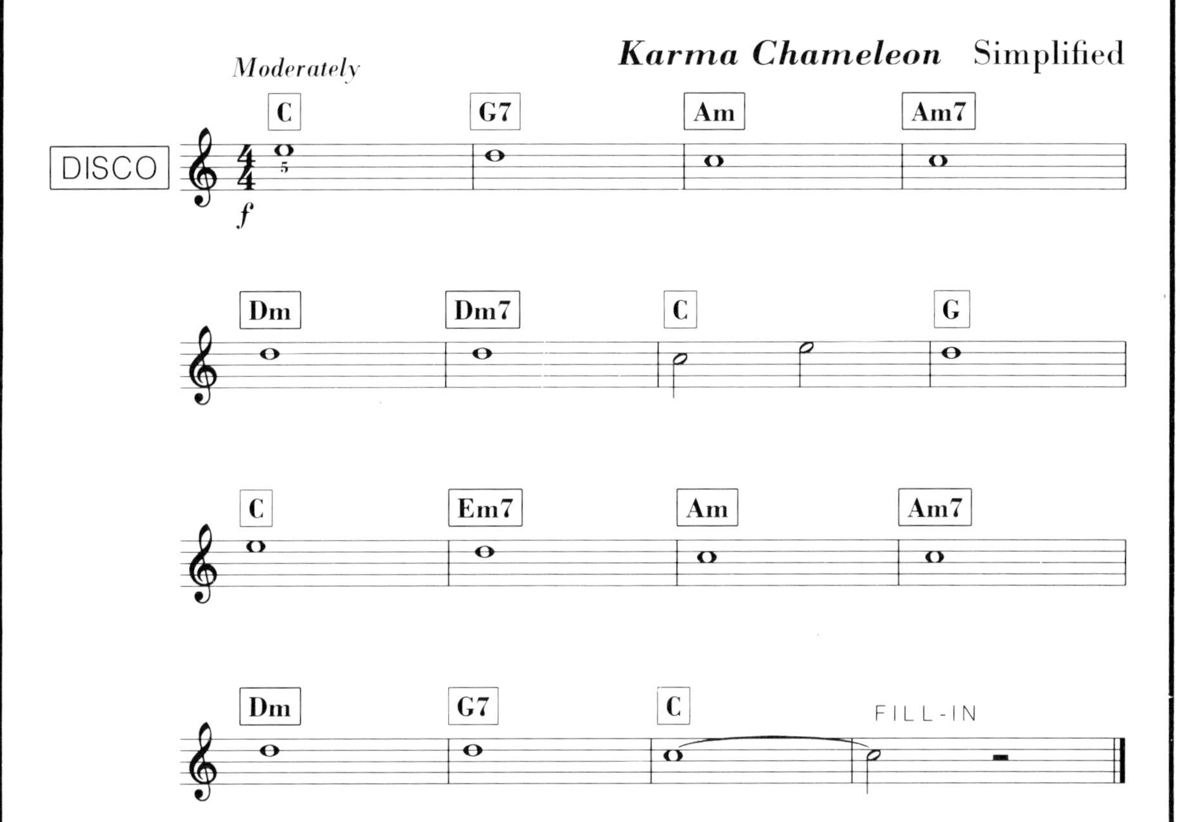

Karma Chameleon Full version

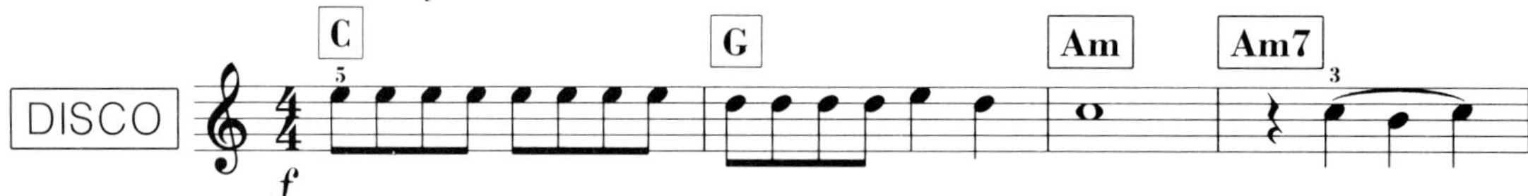

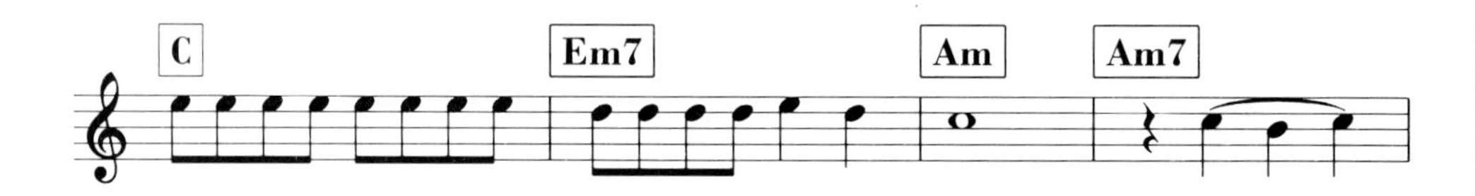

UNIT 3
Exploring rhythm

Semiquavers

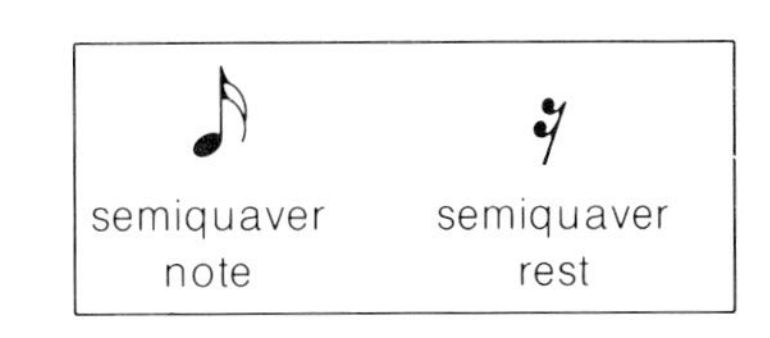

Semiquavers are worth a quarter of a crotchet beat. Sometimes they are called 'sixteenth notes' because there are 16 semiquavers in a $\frac{4}{4}$ bar. Many keyboards have a 16-beat rhythm. Play this rhythm. You will hear the semiquavers played on the cymbals.

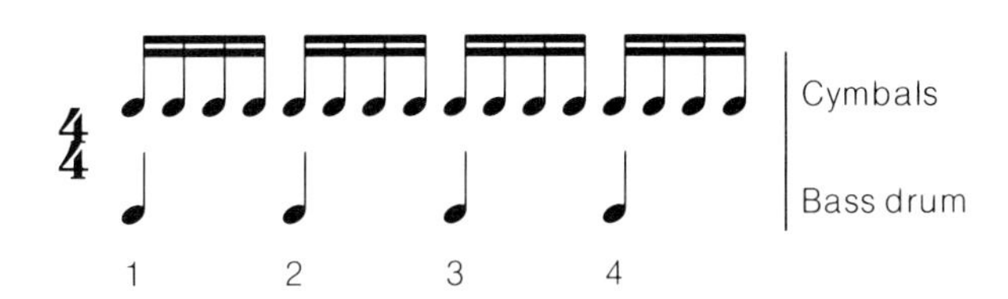

Each group of four semiquavers is worth a crotchet. Use the auto-rhythm to count the beats in these examples. Make sure you play the semiquavers evenly.

What Shall We Do with a Drunken Sailor

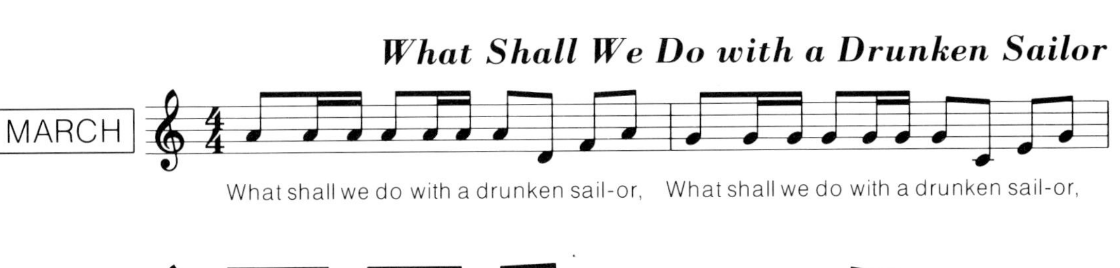

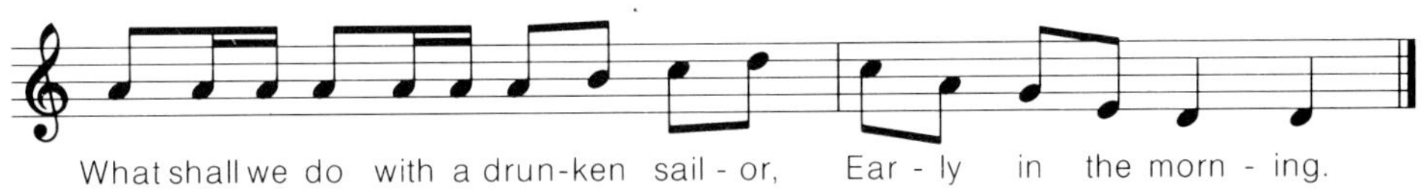

A 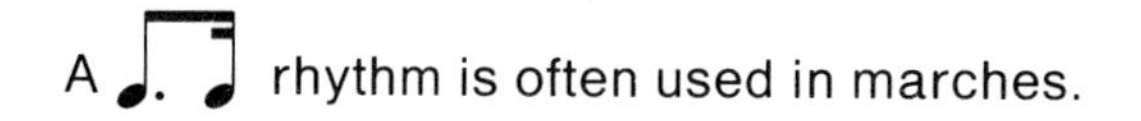 rhythm is often used in marches.

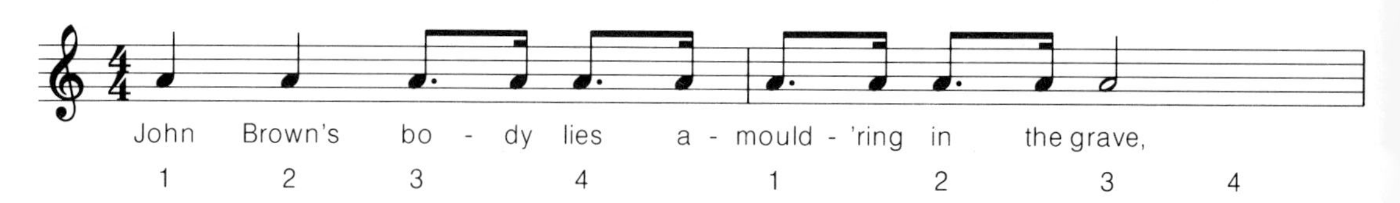

Syncopation

Play this example:

Now play this:

The normal accent of the beat has been moved forward one quaver beat by tying the last two notes. This is called syncopation. Syncopated rhythms are very common in jazz and pop music.

PROJECT WORK

1. Play these two studies slowly to begin with until your fingers can play the notes in time.

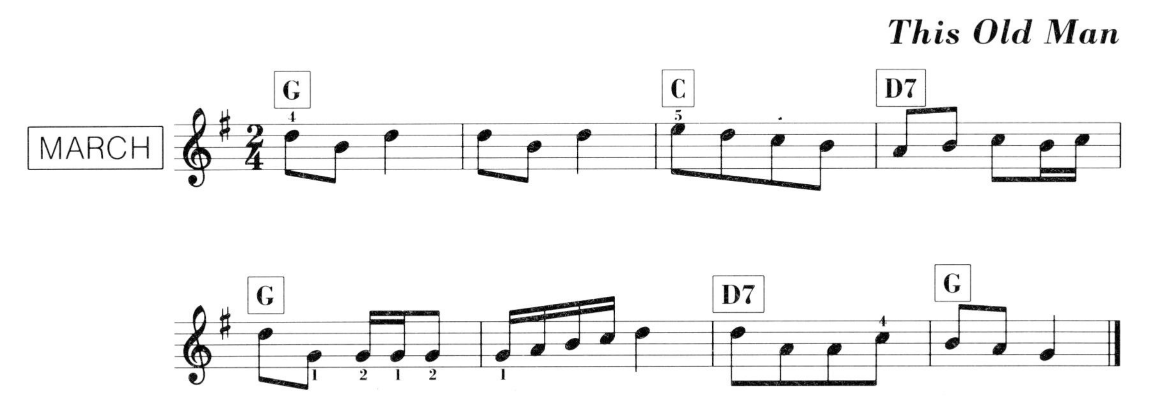

2.

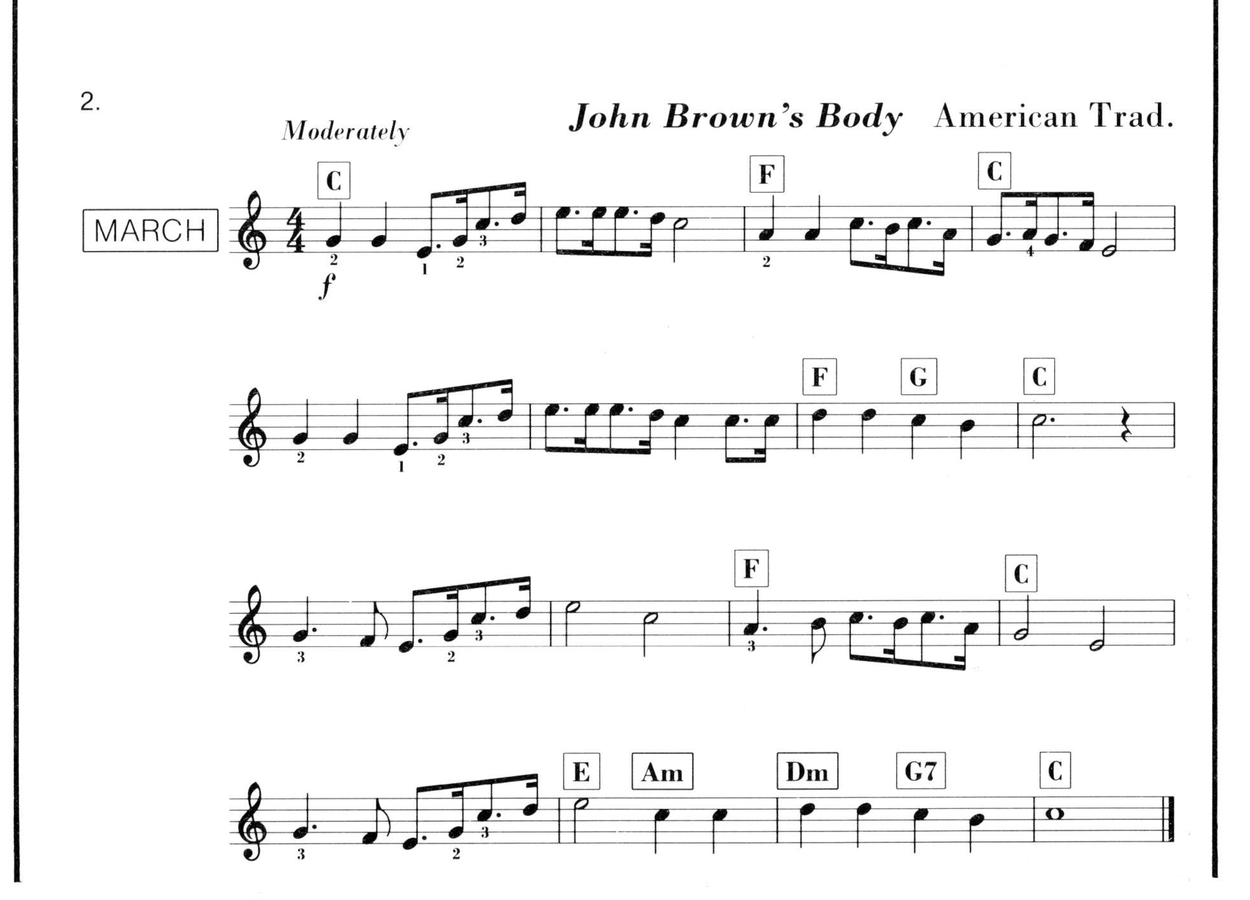

3. Listen to the rhythm on your keyboard and you will get the feel of these two melodies.

La Cucuracha

4.

Mango Walk

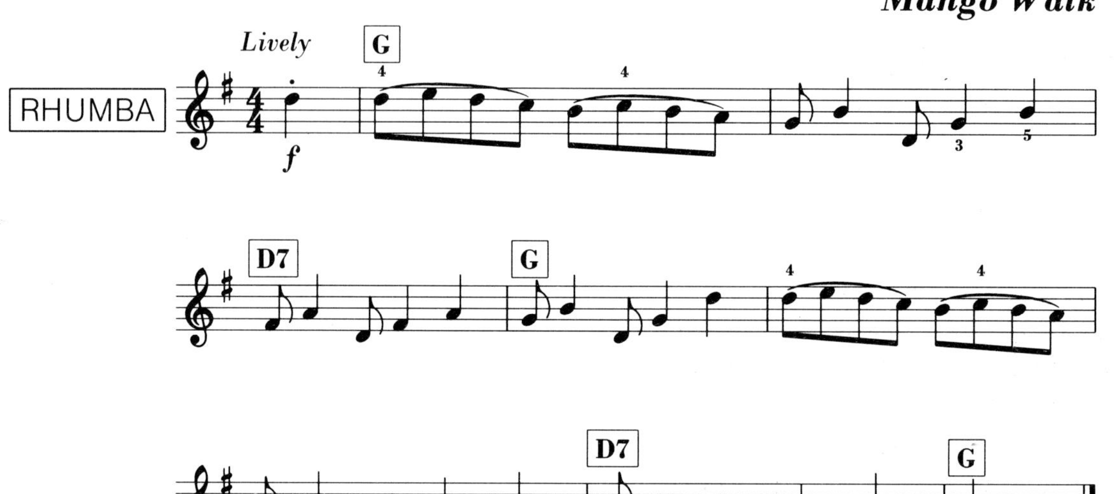

UNIT 4

Melody notes to top C

By adding a few more notes at the top of the stave, you will be able to use two octaves of notes – from middle C to top C.

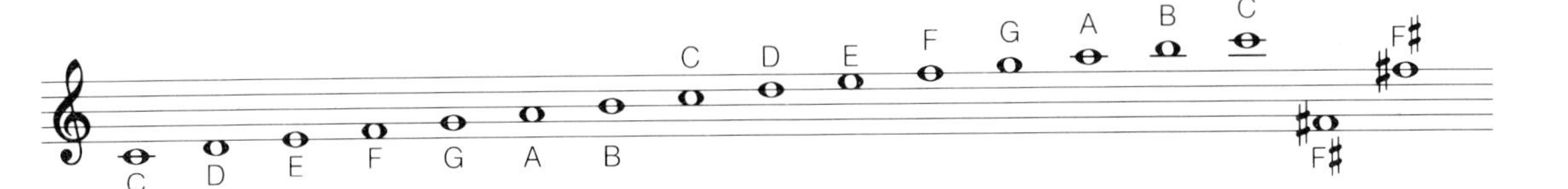

Ledger lines

Notes can be written above and below the stave. The extra lines needed to write these notes are called ledger lines.

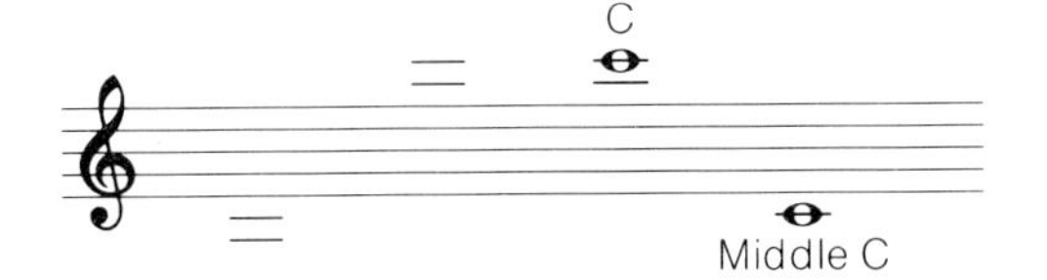

Adding variety to a song

Here are three ways you can add variety to a song.

1. Choose another instrument for each verse.
2. Change the rhythm in the middle section of the verse. Make sure that the rhythms have the same number of beats in a bar.
3. Change key for the last verse. This is easily done if your keyboard has a transposer switch. Just move the control one step up.

PROJECT WORK

1. This tune uses the top end of your keyboard.

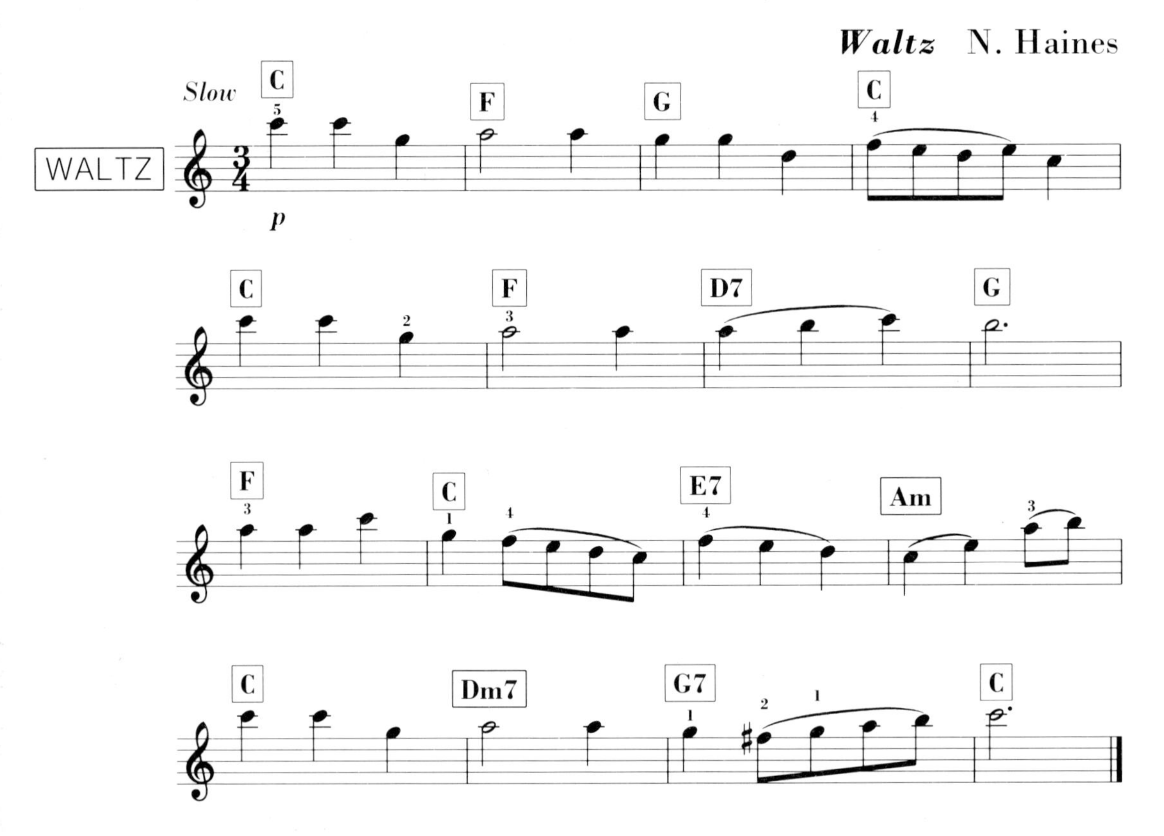

2. Try experimenting with different instruments, rhythms and keys when you repeat back to the beginning.

PROJECT WORK

3. The *Polovtsian Dance No. 1* by Borodin has a middle section that can be highlighted by changing to a swing rhythm. Keep to the same tempo setting. Do not forget the change back to the rhumba rhythm for the return of the main tune.

UNIT 5

Counting in quavers and some keyboard effects

A $\frac{6}{8}$ time signature has six quavers in each bar.

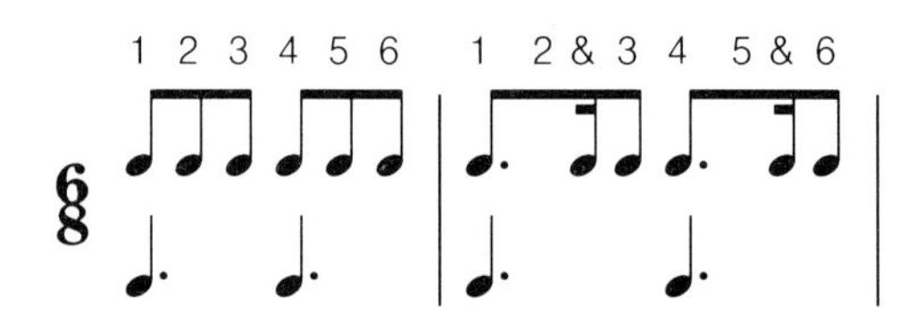

The quavers are grouped in dotted crotchet beats. Try playing the rhythm in time with the words of this limerick. Use any note on the keyboard. Feel the accent on the quaver beats 1 and 4.

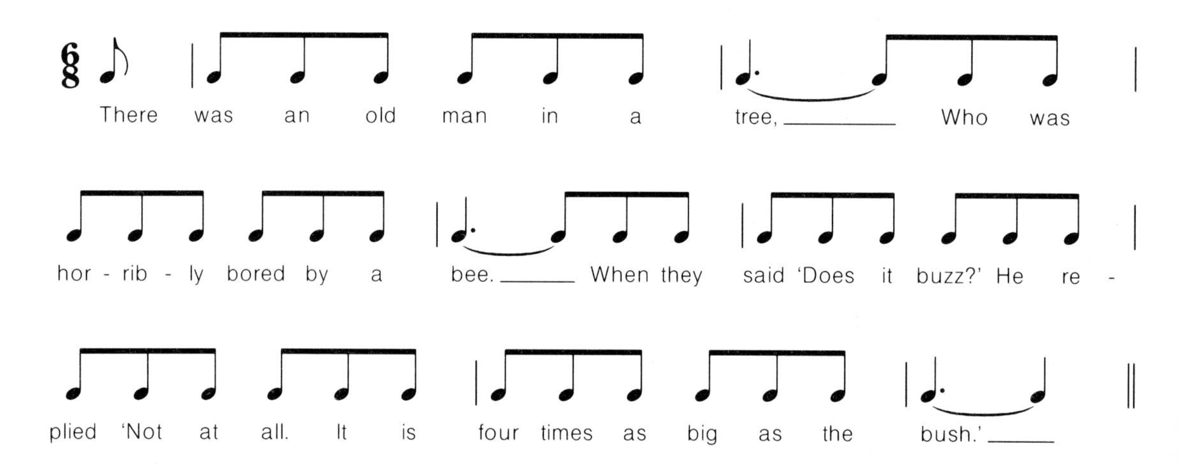

Arpeggio switch

An arpeggio switch is found on most portable keyboards. With this switch on, the notes of the auto-chord are 'spread' up and down the keyboard giving a rippling effect. The arpeggio effect gives you a chordal 'fill-in' from one melody note to another. It is very effective when playing slow music. The arpeggio effect will not work without using the auto-rhythm. Play this chord pattern with the arpeggio effect switched on.

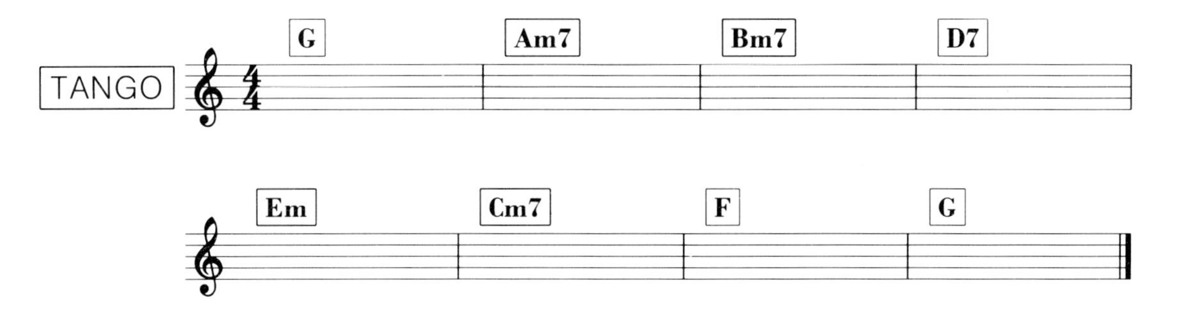

Duet button

With this button pressed down, another note is added automatically under the melody lines. The added notes will fit in with whatever chord is playing on the auto-section of the keyboard. The duet effect will not work without the auto-chord.

With both the arpeggio and duet controls working, the music will sound very full and impressive. Play this melody with the arpeggio and duet effects switched on; then play the same melody without using these effects. Can you hear the difference?

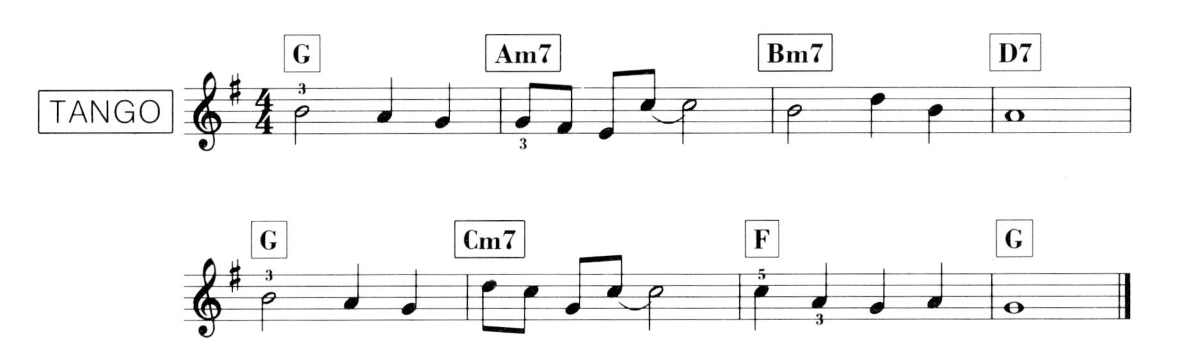

PROJECT WORK

1. When you play these two rhythm exercises, keep counting six quavers in every bar.

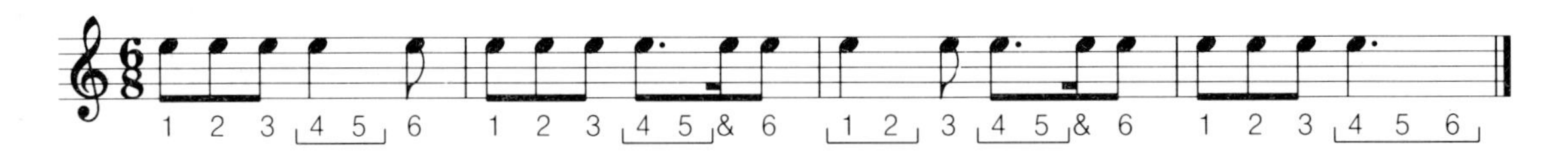

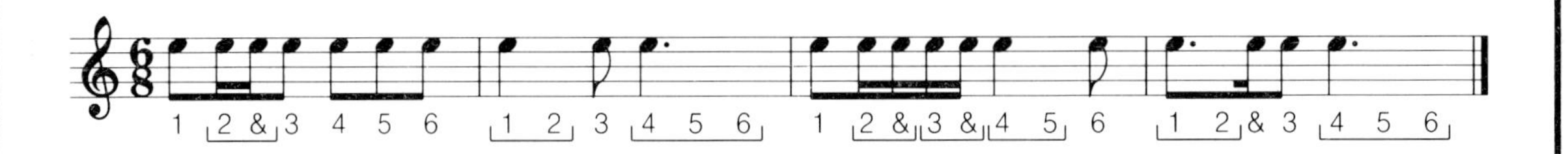

2. FHere are two melodies in $\frac{6}{8}$ time.

Morning from **Peer Gynt** Grieg

Lilliburlero Irish Trad.

3. Use the arpeggio and duet effects when you play this piece. Choose a violin or flute for the melody line.

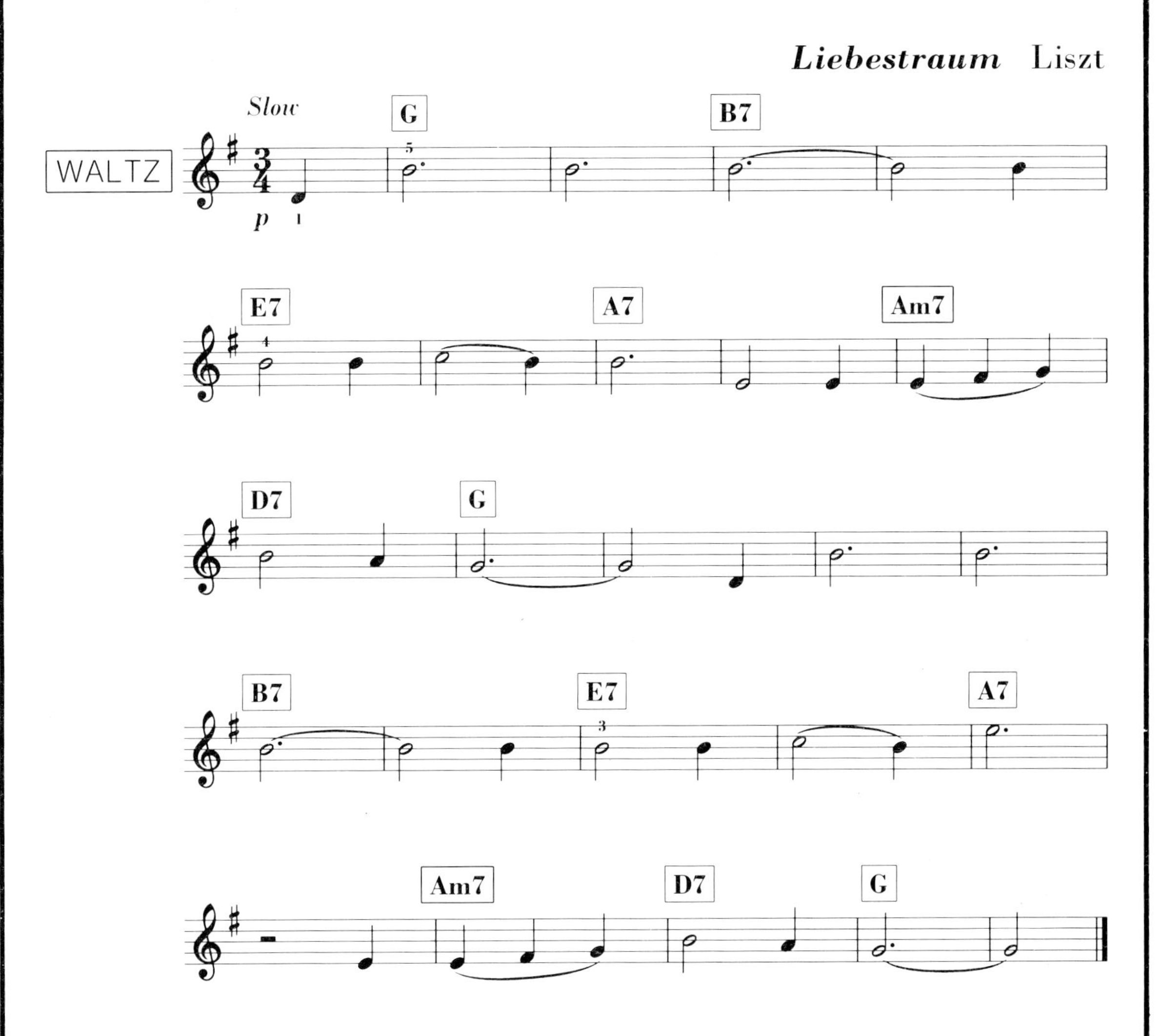

UNIT 6

Accidentals

A flat sign ♭ before a note tells you to play the very next key to the left.

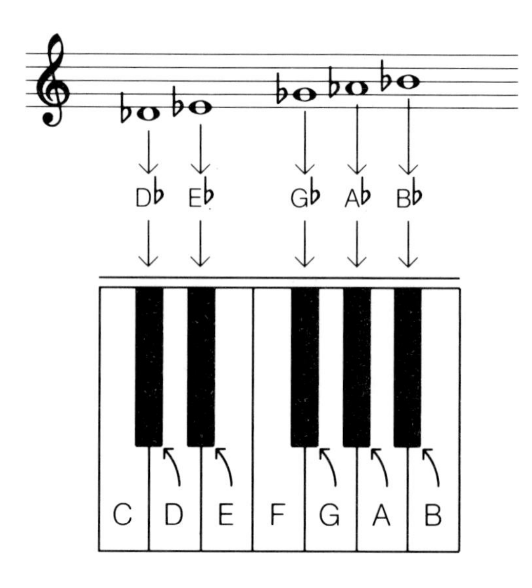

F major has B♭ as its key signature.

Notice that the fingering is different from that of C and G major scales.

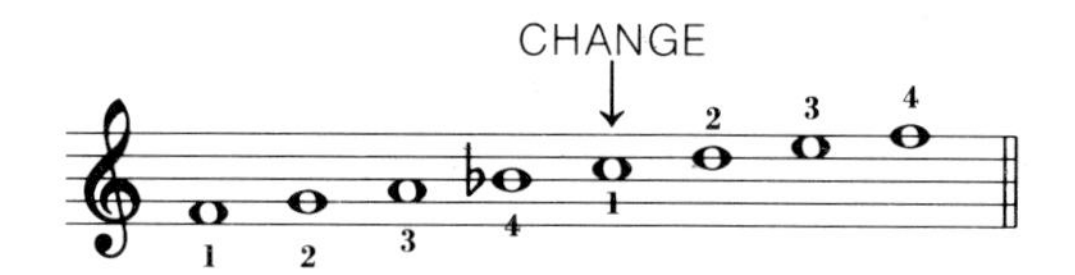

Naturals

A natural sign ♮ before a note cancels out the flat or sharp. A natural note is always a white key.

Flats, naturals, and sharps (which you met in Unit 1) are called accidentals. All accidentals continue to affect the notes in the same position throughout the bar.

You will see that notes can have a sharp or a flat name. For example, F♯ can also be thought of as G♭. The actual name will depend on the key of the music.

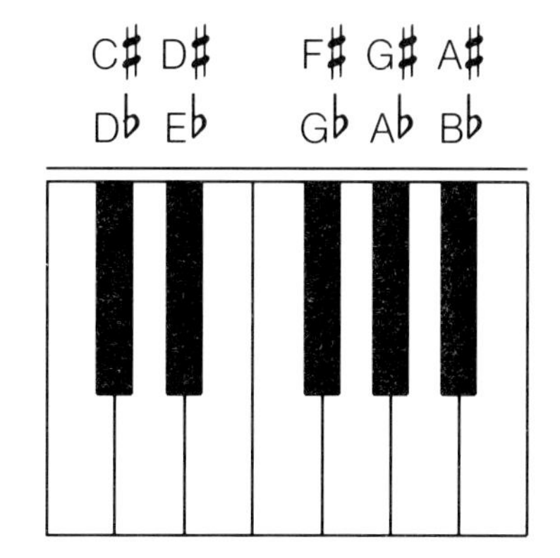

A scale which uses all the white and black notes is called a chromatic scale. The notes are sharpened on the way up, and flattened on the way down.

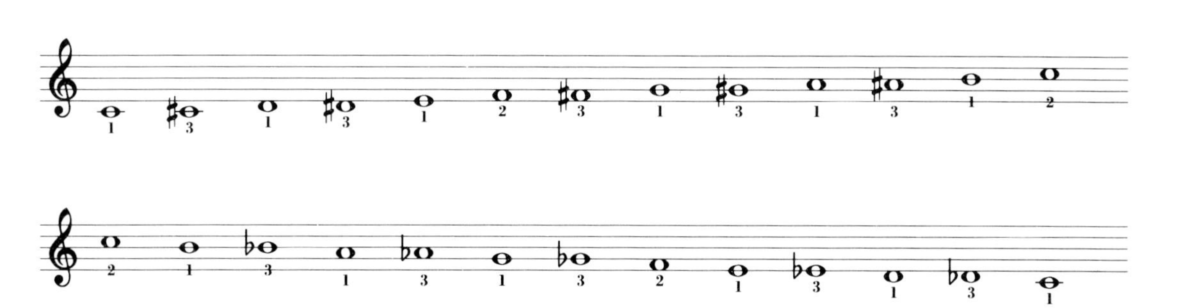

1. This melody has flats, sharps and naturals.

2. Here are two melodies which use accidentals.

Dance of The Sugar Plum Fairy Tchaikovsky

In the Hall of the Mountain King from **Peer Gynt** Greig

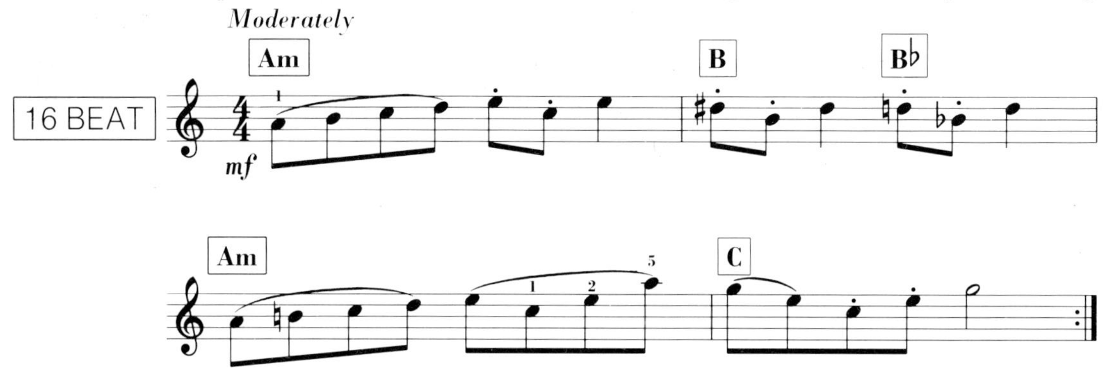

3. Play the quavers in a 'swing' style. The first quaver of each pair should be played slightly longer than its written value. Listen to the swing rhythm and you will get the feel of it.

UNIT 7

Minor keys

Just as there are major and minor chords, so there are major and minor scales. Melodies which are normally major can change character if they are played in the minor key. Play these two versions of *Michael Row the Boat Ashore* and you will hear the difference.

Michael Row the Boat Ashore

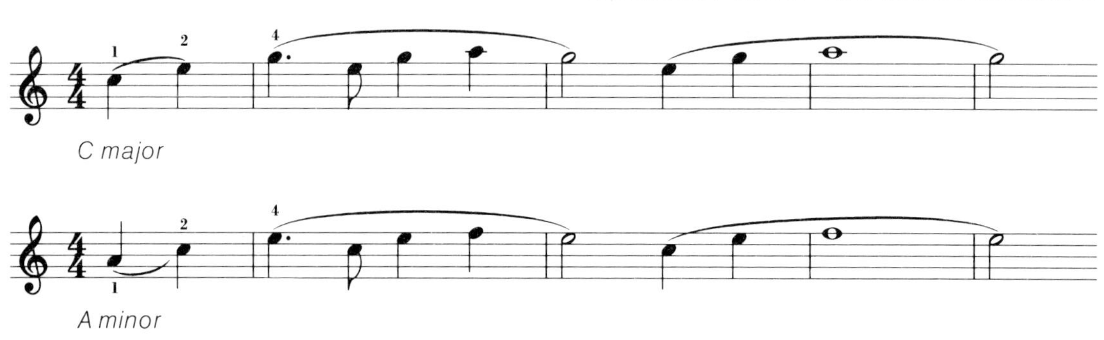

Minor scales usually have the seventh of the scale sharpened. This note is not part of the key signature and has to be added every time the note appears in the music.

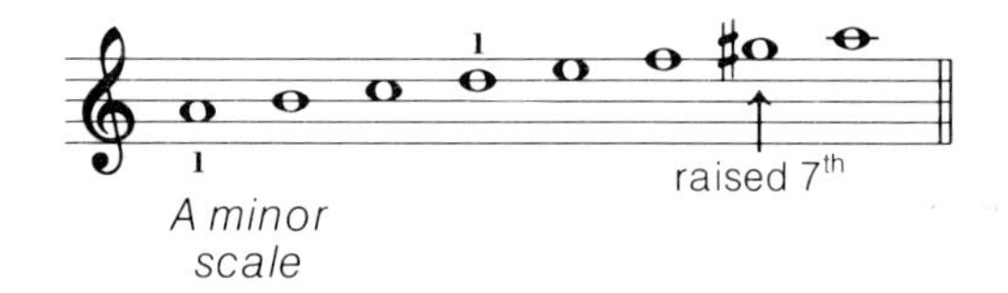

More on auto-chords

Auto-chords based on the black keys are played in the usual way.

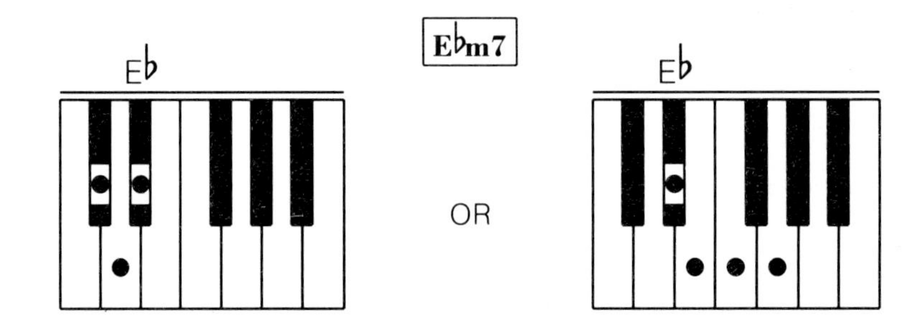

Playing chords with the right hand

So far, you have been playing only one note at a time with the right hand. The auto-chord and rhythm have filled in the rest of the music. If you add notes under the melody, the sound will be much fuller.

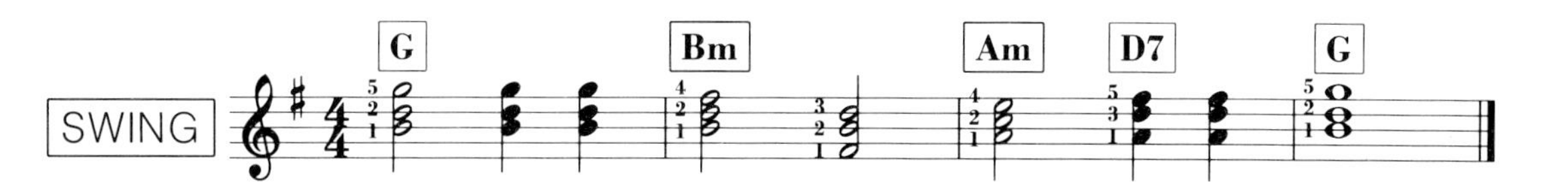

Remember to keep your fingering as smooth as possible. The sustain control is useful to cover up any breaks in the melody.

Terms and signs

Allegro	quickly
Vivace	fast and lively
Moderato	at a moderate pace
Adagio	slowly
Lento	very slowly
D.C.	back to the beginning
Accel.	gradually becoming faster
Rall.	gradually becoming slower
Rit.	hold back
A tempo	at the original speed
Fine	the end of the piece
𝄐	pause

PROJECT WORK

1. Practise the chord patterns in the following piece until each change of auto-chord is smooth and natural. Then play tunes 2. and 3.

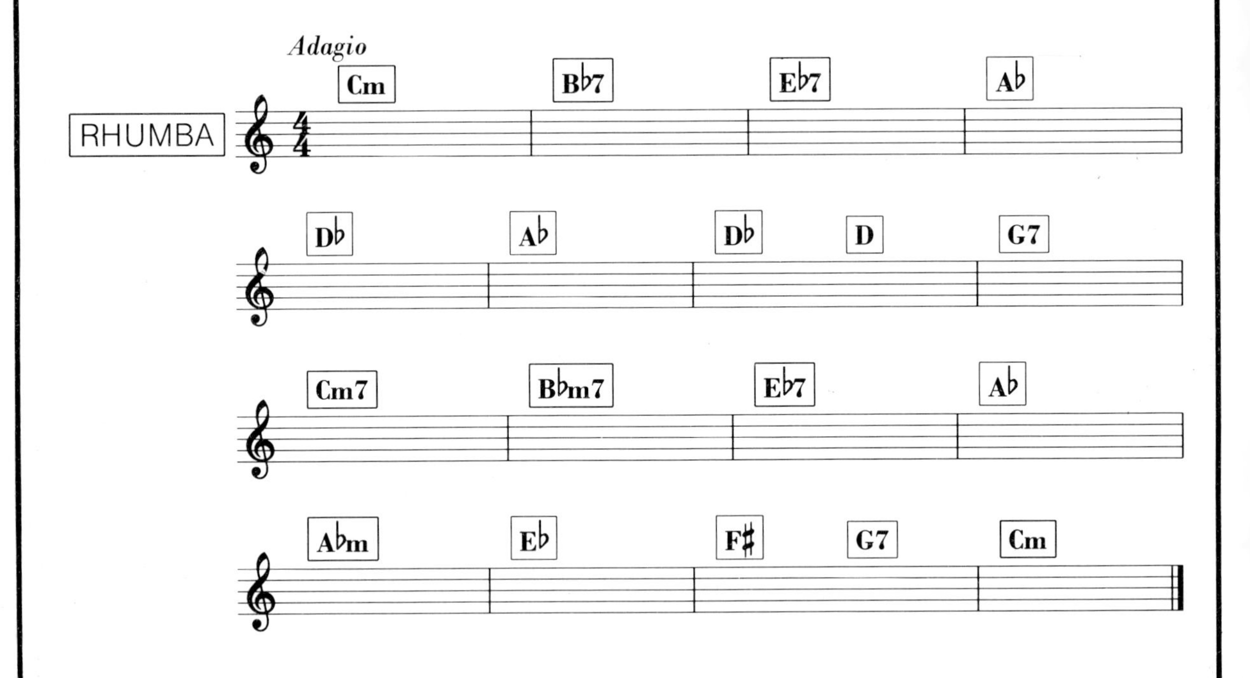

2. *Joshua Fight the Battle of Jericho*

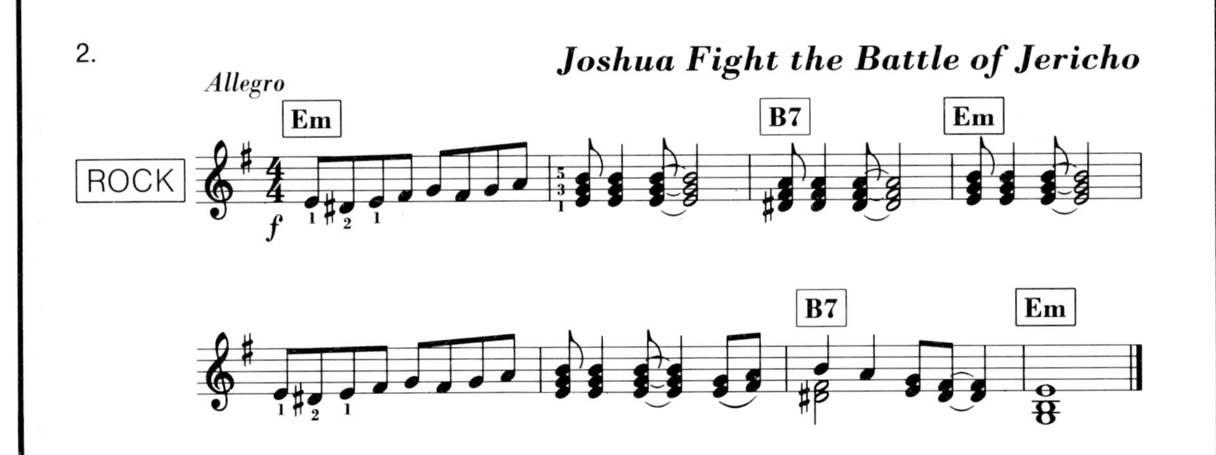

PROJECT WORK
3.
Greensleeves English folksong
Adagio
WALTZ
Am
G
E
F
E7
C
mp
mf
rit.
p

Pieces to play

Canon Pachelbel

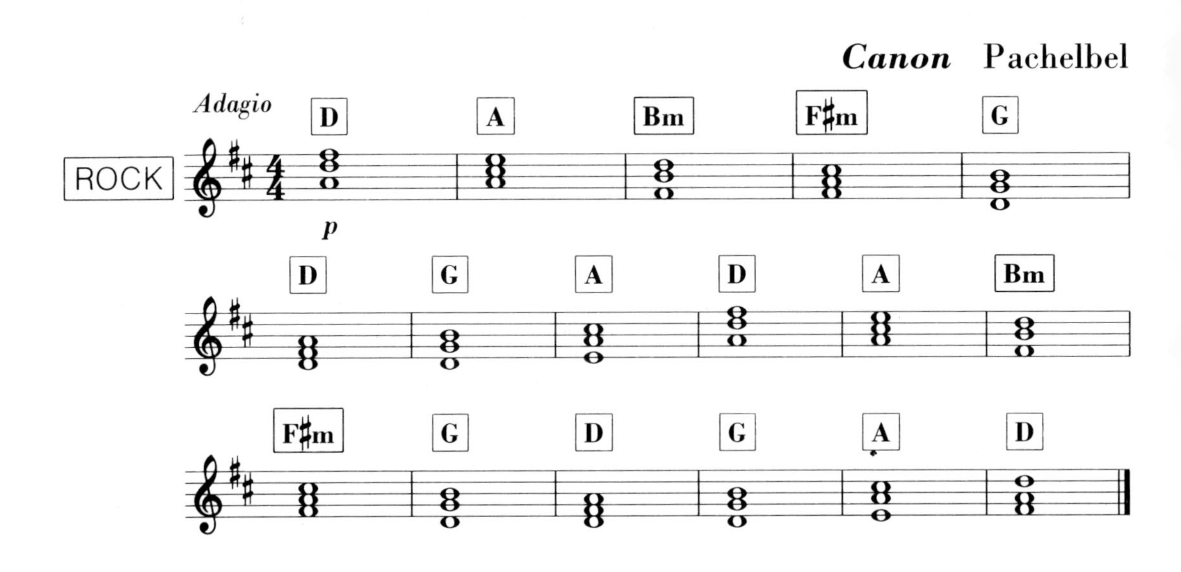

Kum-Ba-Yah

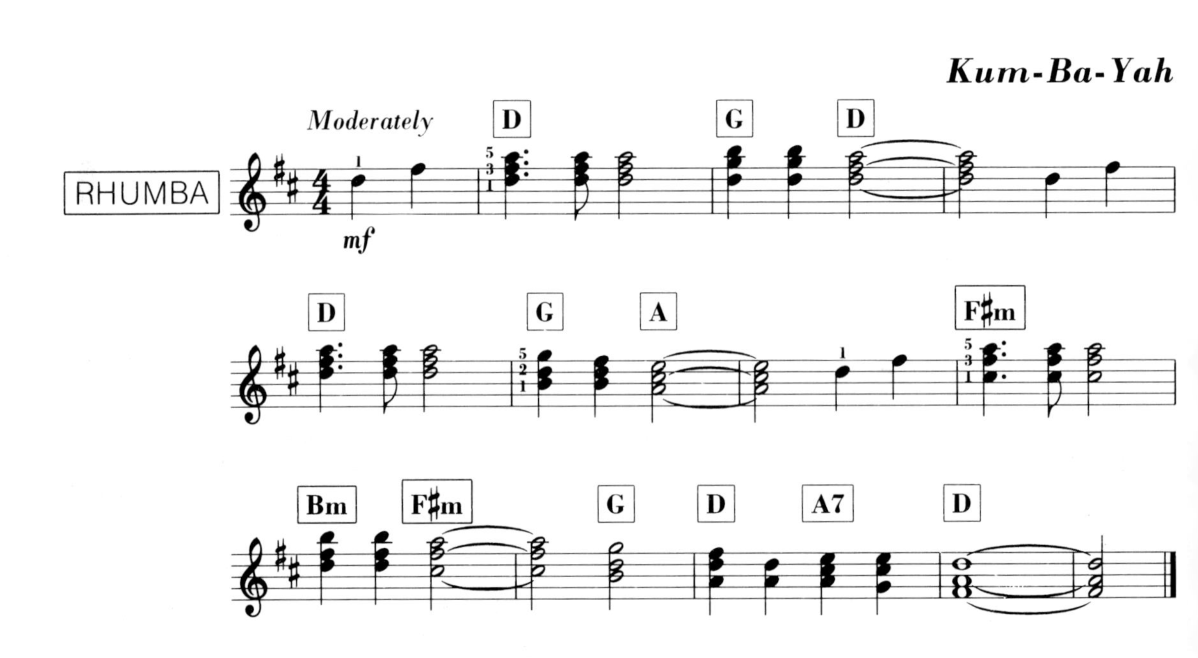

I've Got a Lovely Bunch of Coconuts
Allegro
SLOW ROCK
C
G
The Cancan Offenbach
Allegro
MARCH
D
A7

O Sole Mio di Capua

When I'm 64 The Beatles

Hava Nagila Israeli Trad.

Rondo *Alla Turca* Mozart (arr. N. Haines)

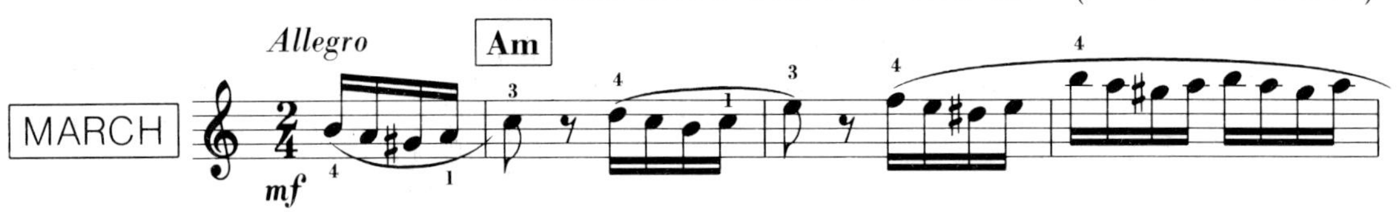

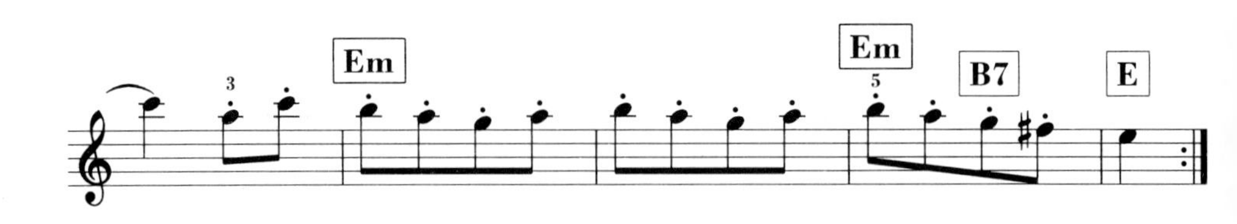

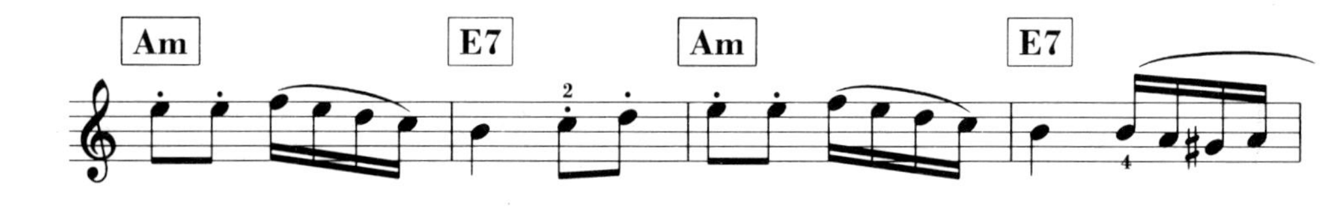

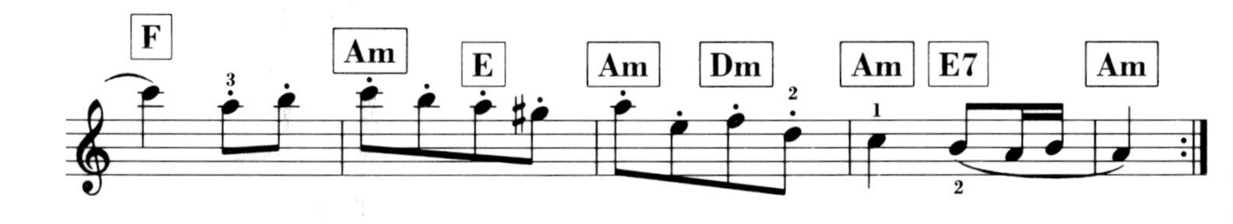

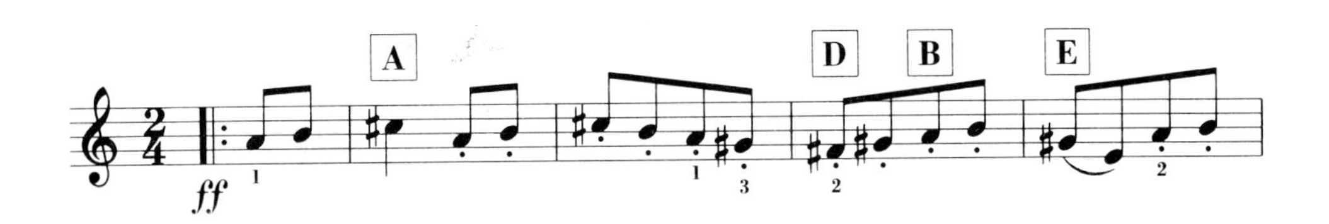
A
D
B
E
ff

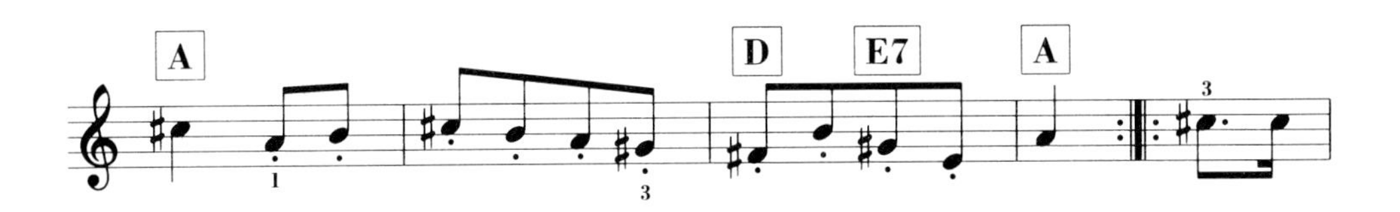
A
D
E7
A

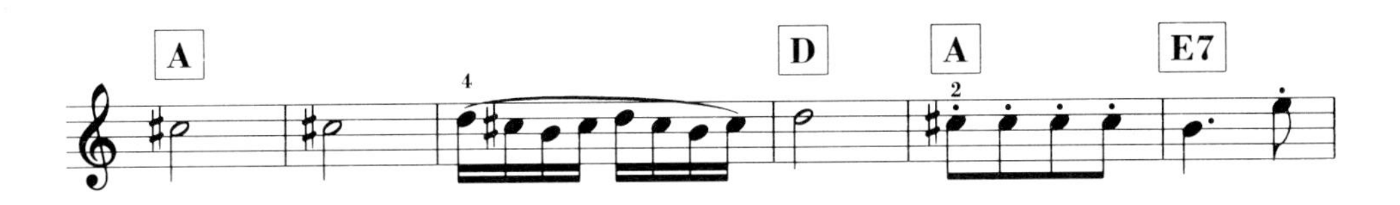
A
D
A
E7

A
D
A
E7
1.
A

2.
A

Waltzing Matilda
Australian Trad.
Moderato
MARCH
F C Dm B♭ F
mf
Gm7 C F C
Dm B♭ F C7 F
f
B♭ F
Gm7 C F C
Dm B♭ F C7 F

Matador Magic

This piece has three sections – A, B, and C. Every section has its own ending called a coda. You can play the piece in a few ways.

1. Play the piece all the way through. The only coda you should play is the one at the end of Section C.

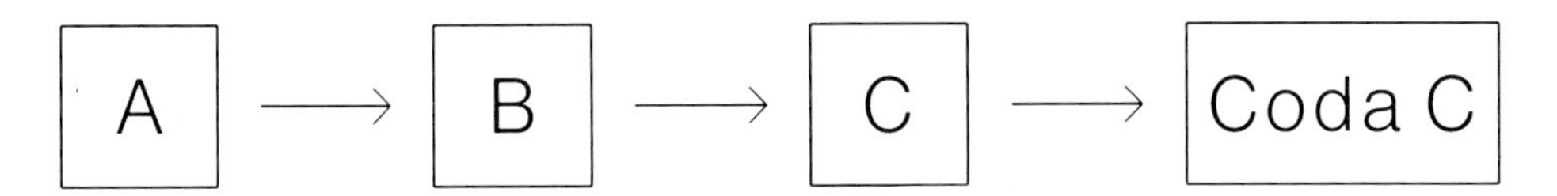

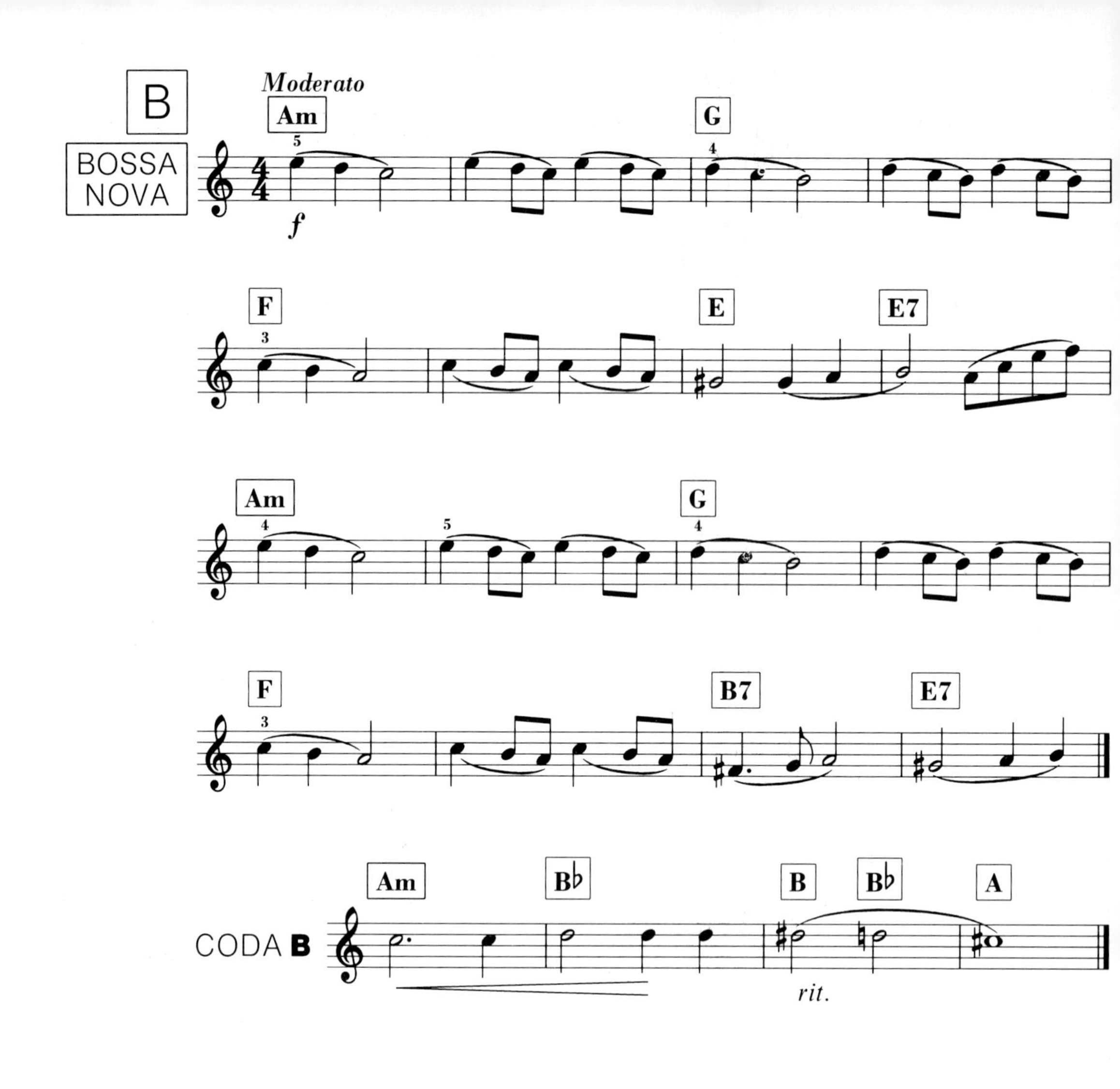
B
BOSSA NOVA
Moderato
Am
G
f
F
E
E7
Am
G
F
B7
E7
CODA B
Am
B♭
B
B♭
A
rit.

C
BOSSA NOVA
Moderato
Am
G
f
F
E
E7

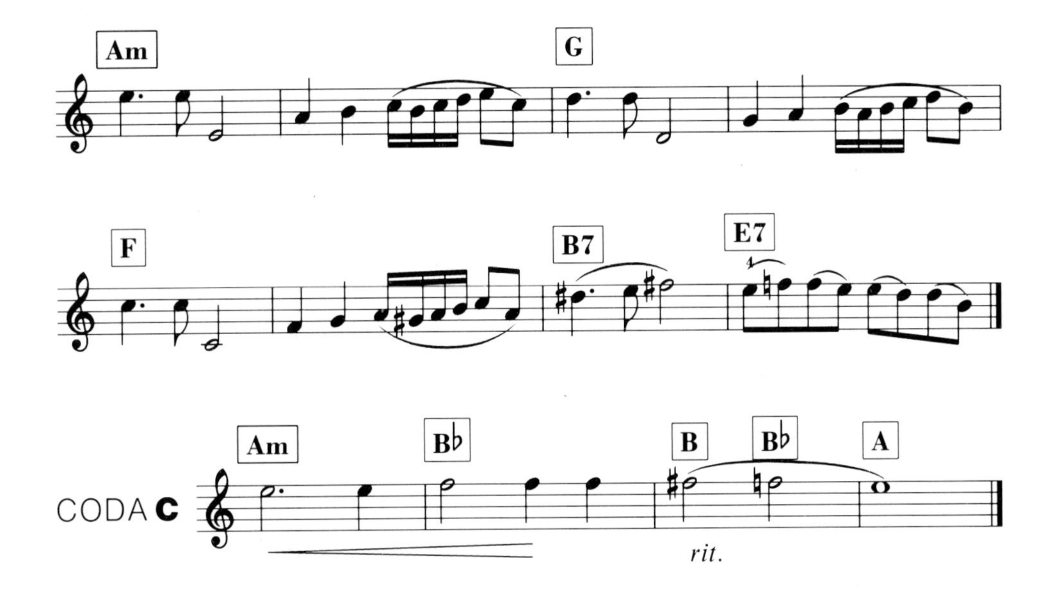

2. *Matador Magic* can also be played by a few keyboard players. Three keyboard groups can be used at the same time with each keyboard group repeating just one of the sections. Only one keyboard should play the auto-chords.

KEYBOARD 1	A → A → A → Coda A
KEYBOARD 2	B → B → B → Coda B
KEYBOARD 3	C → C → C → Coda C

3. Use three keyboard groups. This time, the keyboards should enter one at a time as in a round. Only one keyboard should play the auto-chords.

KEYBOARD 1	A → B → C → A → B → C → Coda C
KEYBOARD 2	A → B → C → A → B → Coda B
KEYBOARD 3	A → B → C → A → Coda A

Study by Chopin (arr. N. Haines)